The Prophetic Woman's Daily Declarations

A 12-Week Journey of Speaking Life, Identity, and Divine Alignment

Prophetess Dr. Racheal Odoy

Giant Publishing Company
Post Office Box 6455
Lincoln, NE 68506
www.giantpublishingcompany.com

Printed in the United States of America.

Scripture quotations are taken from the King James Version of the Bible. This book is intended to inspire, encourage, and equip readers spiritually. It is not a substitute for professional advice or counseling.

ISBN: 979-8-9898098-9-9
Odoy, Racheal

The Prophetic Woman's Daily Declarations
Non-fiction/Racheal Odoy

1. Non-fiction - Christianity
2. Christian living
3. Self-help

Cover design: Prophetess Dr. Racheal Odoy

Also by Prophetess Dr. Racheal Odoy:

You Need a Jonathan
Copyright 2018

I and My Seed will Thrive
Copyright 2019

You Have No Carbon Copy
Copyright 2020

Arise, Woman of Light
Copyright 2025

The Kiss of Death
Copyright 2025

The Power of the Mirror
Copyright 2026

The Devil's Label
Copyright 2026

Winning the Battle for Your Soul
Copyright 2026

DEDICATION

This book is dedicated to every woman
Who has ever questioned her worth…
Who has ever been silenced by fear…
Who has ever carried pain but still showed up with strength.

To the woman who has been overlooked, misunderstood, or broken—
This is for you.

To the mother, the daughter, the leader, the intercessor,
The one who prays in secret and fights battles no one sees—
Heaven sees you.

And Heaven has given you a voice.

May these declarations remind you
Of who you are,
Whose you are,
And what you carry.

You are not ordinary.
You are chosen, called, and anointed.

POEM

There is a voice within you
Not formed by pain,
Not shaped by rejection,
Not defined by what they called you.

It is older than your wounds,
Stronger than your battles,
And deeper than every tear you have cried in secret.

It is the voice of God—
Echoing through your spirit,
Waiting for your agreement.

You were never created to be silent.
You were never designed to shrink.
You were never called to live beneath what Heaven has spoken.

There is a sound that breaks chains,
A declaration that silences fear,
A word that rewrites destinies.

And that sound…
Is in your mouth.

You are not just a woman.
You are a prophetic voice.

Rise.
Speak.
And become.

AUTHOR'S NOTE

There are moments in a woman's life when she begins to believe the wrong voice.

The voice of failure.
The voice of delay.
The voice of past mistakes.
The voice of people who spoke without understanding her destiny.

But there is a greater voice—The voice of God.

"And God said…" *(Genesis 1:3, KJV)*

Everything that exists today began with a declaration.

Light did not appear until God spoke.
Order did not come until God spoke.
Identity was not established until God spoke.

And as women created in His image, we were given the same power—the power of words.

Death and life are in the power of the tongue *(Proverbs 18:21, KJV)*.

This book was birthed from a deep knowing: That many women are living beneath their divine identity. Not because they are not called… But because they are not speaking.

The prophetic is not reserved for a few. It is the voice of God expressed through yielded vessels.

And every day, you have an opportunity to align your life with Heaven through what you say.

These declarations are not mere words.
They are spiritual alignments.
They are seeds.
They are weapons.
They are agreements with God.

As you go through these 12 weeks, do not rush.

Speak slowly.
Speak intentionally.
Speak with faith.

Even when you don't feel it—
Say it.

Even when you don't see it—
Declare it.

Because a prophetic woman does not speak based on her condition…

She speaks based on her covenant.

INTRODUCTION (PART 1)

There is a woman you are becoming.

Not the woman shaped by your past,
Not the woman defined by opinions,
Not the woman limited by fear—

But the woman God spoke about before you were ever born.

"Before I formed thee in the belly I knew thee…" *(Jeremiah 1:5, KJV)*

You are not discovering yourself.
You are remembering who God said you are.

This journey is not about trying harder.
It is about aligning deeper.

Every day you speak,
You are either agreeing with Heaven…
Or reinforcing what life has told you.

And many women, unknowingly, have been prophesying limitations over their own lives.

"I am tired."
"I am not enough."
"Nothing is working."
"Maybe this is just how my life is."

These are not just statements.
They are declarations.

And declarations shape outcomes.

INTRODUCTION (PART 2)

But there is another way.

A prophetic woman speaks differently.

She speaks life in the middle of dryness.
She speaks hope in the middle of uncertainty.
She speaks identity in the middle of confusion.

She calls those things which be not as though they were *(Romans 4:17, KJV)*.

This book is an invitation.

An invitation to come into agreement with God.
An invitation to take authority over your words.
An invitation to step into the woman you were always meant to be.

You will not leave this journey the same.

Because as you speak daily—
Something within you will begin to shift.

Your thoughts will change.
Your confidence will rise.
Your identity will become clearer.

And slowly… but surely…
You will begin to see yourself the way God sees you.

HOW TO USE THIS BOOK

(PART 1)

This book is not meant to be rushed.
It is meant to be walked through—day by day, word by word, declaration by declaration.

The Prophetic Woman's Daily Declarations is a 12-week journey designed to align your voice, your thoughts, and your spirit with what God has spoken concerning your life.

Each day is intentional.
Each word is purposeful.
Each declaration is an invitation to come into agreement with Heaven.

This is more than a devotional.
This is a daily encounter.

Every day you engage with this book, you are not just reading—you are participating.

You are speaking.
You are agreeing.
You are becoming.

HOW TO USE THIS BOOK

(PART 2)

Each day is structured to guide you into a complete spiritual experience:

You will begin with **Scripture**, because everything is built on the Word of God. His Word is truth, and it establishes your foundation.

You will then move into a **Reflection**, where the Scripture is brought to life in a simple and meaningful way.

After that comes the **Prophetic Declaration**—the heart of each day.
This is where you use your voice.

As you declare, you are:
Aligning with God,
Shifting atmospheres,
Releasing truth, and establishing what Heaven has already spoken.

You will then enter into a **Prayer**, connecting personally with God.

And finally, a **Reflection Question** will help you go deeper and apply what you have received.

HOW TO USE THIS BOOK

(PART 3)

To receive the fullness of this journey:

Speak out loud.
Your voice carries power. There is authority in what you say.

Be consistent.
Even when you do not feel it—show up.

Believe what you are declaring.
Faith gives life to your words.

Take your time.
Do not rush through the days. Let each one minister to you.

Repeat when necessary.
Some days may speak to you more deeply—return to them if needed.

There will be days when your emotions do not agree with what you are declaring.

Still—speak.

Because a prophetic woman does not speak based on how she feels…
She speaks based on truth.

HOW TO USE THIS BOOK

(PART 4)

As you continue through these 12 weeks, you will begin to notice change.

Not suddenly—but steadily.
Not loudly—but deeply.

Your thoughts will begin to shift.
Your confidence will begin to rise.
Your identity will become clearer.

You will start to recognize your voice again.

Life and death are in the power of the tongue *(Proverbs 18:21, KJV)*.

Your words are not empty.
They are seeds.

And every day, you are planting something.

Let it be life.
Let it be truth.
Let it be what God has said.

Approach this journey with expectation.

God is present.
And as you speak His Word daily—
You are not just declaring…

You are becoming.

TABLE OF CONTENTS

Week 1: Identity — Knowing Who You Are in God

Week 2: Healing — Restoring the Inner Woman

Week 3: Faith — Trusting God Completely

Week 9: Finances & Provision – Trusting God as Your Source

Week 10: Health & Wholeness – Caring for the Whole Woman

Week 11: Spiritual Authority & Growth – Walking in Power and Maturity

Week 12: Victory & Dominion – Living Above and Not Beneath

Identity

Knowing Who You Are in God

Anchor Scripture (KJV)

"But ye are a chosen generation, a royal priesthood, an holy nation, a peculiar people…"
— *1 Peter 2:9*

EXHORTATION

Identity is the foundation of everything.

How you see yourself will determine how you speak, how you respond, what you accept, and what you believe is possible for your life.

Many women are not struggling because they lack ability…
They are struggling because they have believed the wrong identity.

Life has a way of placing labels on people—
Through experiences, through words spoken in pain, through rejection, through delay.

But those labels are not truth.

God already defined you before life tried to redefine you.

You are not what happened to you.
You are not what people said about you.
You are not your past.

You are who God says you are.

This week is a return.

A return to truth.
A return to identity.

A return to what has always been written about you in Heaven.

You will begin to unlearn every false label…
And step into the truth of who you are.

Not gradually alone—but intentionally, daily, through your words.

Because what you repeatedly say—

You eventually believe. And what you believe—You eventually become.

Day 1

I Am Known by God

Scripture (KJV)

"O Lord, thou hast searched me, and known me."
— *Psalm 139:1*

Reflection

There is something deeply comforting about being known.

Not partially.
Not in fragments.
But fully.

God does not know a version of you—He knows all of you.
Every thought, every fear, every desire, every hidden place.

Nothing about you surprises Him.
Nothing about you confuses Him.

And still… He loves you.

You do not have to perform to be seen.
You do not have to pretend to be strong.

You are already known.
And you are already loved.

Prophetic Declaration

I declare that I am fully known by God.
Nothing about me is hidden from Him, and nothing about me disqualifies me.

I am seen.
I am understood.
I am loved without condition.

God is mindful of me, and my life matters.

Prayer

Father, thank You for knowing me completely.
Thank You that I do not have to hide or pretend before You.

Help me to rest in Your love and to trust that I am safe in You.

In Jesus' name, Amen.

Reflection Question

Do I truly believe that God knows me and still loves me?

Day 2

I Am Chosen

Scripture (KJV)

"Ye have not chosen me, but I have chosen you…"
— *John 15:16*

Reflection

To be chosen is to be wanted.

Not as an afterthought.
Not as a second option.
But intentionally.

God did not choose you randomly.
He chose you on purpose.

Before you ever tried to prove yourself,
Before you ever felt qualified—
He had already chosen you.

You are not overlooked in Heaven.
You are selected.

Prophetic Declaration

I declare that I am chosen by God.
I am not rejected, forgotten, or overlooked.

My life has purpose.
My calling is intentional.
I have been selected for such a time as this.

Prayer

Lord, thank You for choosing me.
Help me to walk confidently in the calling You have placed on my life.

Remove every feeling of rejection
And replace it with the assurance of Your choice.

In Jesus' name,
Amen.

Reflection Question

Where have I felt rejected, and how can I replace that with the truth that I am chosen?

Day 3

I Am Loved

Scripture (KJV)

"I have loved thee with an everlasting love…"
—*Jeremiah 31:3*

Reflection

God's love is not temporary.
It does not change with your performance.

It is not based on how well you are doing.
It is not withdrawn when you make mistakes.

His love is constant.
Steady.
Unchanging.

There is nothing you can do to make Him love you more…
And nothing you can do to make Him love you less.

You are already loved—fully and completely.

Prophetic Declaration

I declare that I am deeply loved by God.
His love for me is constant and unchanging.

I am not striving for love—
I am living from it.

I receive His love fully and without fear.

Prayer

Father, thank You for Your everlasting love.
Help me to receive it fully
And to walk in the confidence of being loved by You.

In Jesus' name,
Amen.

Reflection Question

Do I live like I am loved by God, or do I still feel like I have to earn it?

Day 4

I Am Accepted

Scripture (KJV)

"To the praise of the glory of his grace, wherein he hath made us accepted in the beloved."
— *Ephesians 1:6*

Reflection

Acceptance is something many people spend their lives searching for.

To belong.
To be embraced.
To feel like they are enough.

But God did not create you to chase acceptance— He already gave it to you.

You are not trying to be accepted by God.
You already are.

Not because of perfection.
Not because of performance.

But because of His grace.

You belong to Him.
And in Him—you are fully accepted.

Prophetic Declaration

I declare that I am accepted by God.
I do not have to strive, perform, or prove myself.

I belong.
I am embraced.
I am enough through Christ.

I walk boldly in the confidence of divine acceptance.

Prayer

Father, thank You that I am accepted in You.
Break every mindset that makes me feel like I have to earn Your love.

Help me to rest in the truth
That I already belong.

In Jesus' name,
Amen.

Reflection Question

Where in my life am I still trying to earn acceptance instead of resting in it?

Day 5

I Am Redeemed

Scripture (KJV)

"In whom we have redemption through his blood, the forgiveness of sins, according to the riches of his grace."
— *Ephesians 1:7*

Reflection

Redemption means you have been bought back.

Not because you were worthless—
But because you were valuable.

There may be things in your past you wish you could change.
Moments you regret.
Decisions you would undo if you could.

But God does not relate to you based on your past.
He relates to you through redemption.

Your past is not your identity.
Your mistakes are not your definition.
You have been forgiven.

You have been restored.
You have been made new.

Prophetic Declaration

I declare that I am redeemed by the blood of Jesus.
My past does not define me.

I am forgiven.
I am restored.
I am made new.

I walk in freedom, not in shame.
I embrace the grace that has been given to me.

Prayer

Father, thank You for redeeming me.
Thank You for Your grace that covers my past.

Help me to walk in the freedom You have given me
And to let go of every form of guilt and shame.

In Jesus' name, Amen.

Reflection Question

Am I still holding onto guilt that God has already forgiven?

Day 6

I Am Set Apart

Scripture (KJV)

"But ye are a chosen generation, a royal priesthood, an holy nation, a peculiar people…"
— *1 Peter 2:9*

Reflection

Being set apart does not mean you are strange—
It means you are intentional.

God did not call you to blend in.
He called you to stand out.

There is a difference on your life.
A calling.
A distinction.

And sometimes, that difference can feel uncomfortable.

You may feel misunderstood.
You may feel like you do not fully fit in certain spaces.

But that is not rejection—it is identity.

You are set apart for a purpose.

Prophetic Declaration

I declare that I am set apart by God.
I embrace the uniqueness of who He has called me to be.

I am not pressured to conform.
I walk boldly in my divine identity.

I am chosen, called, and separated for His purpose.

Prayer

Lord, thank You for setting me apart.
Help me to embrace my identity without fear or comparison.

Give me the boldness to walk confidently
In the life You have called me to live.

In Jesus' name,
Amen.

Reflection Question

Have I ever mistaken being set apart for being rejected?

Day 7

I Am God's Masterpiece

Scripture (KJV)

"For we are his workmanship, created in Christ Jesus unto good works, which God hath before ordained that we should walk in them."
— *Ephesians 2:10*

Reflection

You are not an accident. You are not a mistake.

You are not a collection of flaws that God is trying to fix.

You are His workmanship – His Masterpiece. Before you took your first breath, God already knew you. He designed you with purpose, beauty, and destiny. Every gift, every strength, every lesson, and even every challenge have been woven into the story He is writing through your life.

The enemy often tries to make women focus on what they lack. God wants you to focus on who you are in Him. When you see yourself through God's eyes, insecurity begins to lose its power. You were created intentionally. You were created purposefully. You were created beautifully. And God is still working in you.

Prophetic Declaration

I declare that I am God's masterpiece. I am fearfully and wonderfully made.

I reject every lie that says I am not enough. I embrace the woman God created me to be.

I walk confidently in His purpose for my life. I am valuable, chosen, and deeply loved by God.

Prayer

Father, thank You for creating me with purpose and intention. Help me to see myself through Your eyes and not through the opinions of others.

Remove every insecurity, fear, and false belief that has tried to define me. Teach me to walk confidently in the identity You have given me. May my life reflect the beauty of Your workmanship.

In Jesus' name, Amen.

Reflection Question

What negative belief about myself do I need to replace with God's truth today?

Week 1 Closing

You have completed Week 1.

You have begun to see yourself differently.

Not through past experiences—
But through truth.

Identity is no longer uncertain.
It is becoming established.

What you have declared this week
Is taking root within you.

And as you continue—
You will no longer question who you are.

You will walk in it.

Prophetic Charge

I know who I am.
I walk confidently in my identity.

Week 2

Healing-
Restoring the
Inner Woman

Anchor Scripture (KJV)

"He healeth the broken in heart, and bindeth up their wounds."
— *Psalm 147:3*

EXHORTATION

PART 1

Healing is not weakness.
Healing is strength.

There are wounds that are visible—
And there are wounds that are hidden.

The hidden ones are often the deepest.

Words spoken years ago…
Moments of rejection…
Betrayal you did not expect…
Disappointments that left questions in your heart…

These things do not always leave your life—
But they can leave marks within you.

And if left unattended,
They begin to shape how you think, how you trust, and how you see yourself.

EXHORTATION

PART 2

But God is not intimidated by your wounds.

He does not avoid broken places—
He restores them.

Healing is not pretending something didn't happen.
Healing is allowing God to touch what happened
And remove its power over you.

This week is an invitation.

An invitation to release what you have carried.
An invitation to confront what you have avoided.
An invitation to allow God to heal—not just outwardly, but inwardly.

EXHORTATION

PART 3

You do not have to remain defined by pain.

You do not have to carry what God is ready to heal.

There is grace for your healing.
There is peace available to you.
There is restoration waiting.

And as you speak this week—
Healing will not just be something you hope for…

It will be something you begin to experience.

WEEKLY PROPHETIC PRAYER

Father, in the name of Jesus,

I bring every hidden wound before You.
Every pain I have carried silently,
Every hurt I have not fully released—

I surrender it to You.

Heal my heart.
Restore my soul.
Remove every weight that is not from You.

Where there has been pain, bring peace.
Where there has been brokenness, bring wholeness.
Where there has been confusion, bring clarity.

I receive Your healing fully.

In Jesus' name,
Amen.

WEEKLY AFFIRMATION

I am healing.
I am whole.
I am being restored by God.

My past does not control me.
God is restoring every part of my life.

Day 8

Healing from Past Pain

Scripture (KJV)

"He restoreth my soul…"
— *Psalm 23:3*

Reflection

Pain has a way of lingering.

Even when life moves forward,
Some experiences remain within us.

Things we thought we had moved past…
But somehow still affect how we feel, how we respond, and how we trust.

But God is not asking you to ignore your pain—
He is inviting you to release it.

You were not created to carry pain forever.
You were created to be restored.

Prophetic Declaration

I declare that I am healing from every past pain.

What hurt me will not define me.
What wounded me will not control me.

God is restoring my soul.
I release every burden and receive His healing.

Prayer

Father, I give You every pain from my past.
Every hurt I have held onto—knowingly or unknowingly.

Restore my soul.
Heal every place within me that still carries pain.

In Jesus' name,
Amen.

Reflection Question

What pain have I been carrying that I need to release to God?

Day 9

Freedom from Rejection

Scripture (KJV)

"The Lord hath appeared of old unto me, saying,
Yea, I have loved thee with an everlasting love…"
— *Jeremiah 31:3*

Reflection

Rejection has a voice.

It tells you that you are not enough.
That you were overlooked.
That you were not chosen.

And if not dealt with,
It begins to shape how you see yourself.

But rejection from people
Does not mean rejection from God.

God's love for you has never changed.
And His acceptance of you is not based on human response.

You are not rejected.
You are loved.

Prophetic Declaration

I declare that I am free from every spirit of rejection.

I am loved by God with an everlasting love.
I am not overlooked.
I am not forgotten.

I reject every lie that says I am not enough.

Prayer

Father, heal every place where I have felt rejected.

Remove every lie that formed in those moments
And replace it with Your truth.

Help me to see myself as loved and chosen.

In Jesus' name,
Amen.

Reflection Question

How has rejection affected the way I see myself?

Day 10

Letting Go of Hurt

Scripture (KJV)

"Let all bitterness, and wrath, and anger… be put away from you…"
— *Ephesians 4:31*

Reflection

Hurt has a way of holding on.

Even when the moment has passed,
The feeling can remain.

And sometimes, without realizing it,
We carry hurt into new seasons, new relationships, and new opportunities.

But what you carry can begin to weigh you down.

God is not asking you to pretend it didn't happen—
He is asking you to release it.

Letting go is not weakness.
It is freedom.

Prophetic Declaration

I declare that I release every hurt I have been holding onto.

I let go of bitterness, anger, and pain.
I refuse to carry what God is asking me to release.

I walk in freedom, peace, and emotional healing.

Prayer

Father, I release every hurt to You.

Every memory that still carries pain—
I place it in Your hands.

Help me to let go fully
And to walk in the freedom You have given me.

In Jesus' name,
Amen.

Reflection Question

What am I holding onto that God is asking me to release?

Day 11

Healing from Betrayal

Scripture (KJV)

"It was not an enemy that reproached me… but it was thou, a man mine equal…"
— *Psalm 55:12–13*

Reflection

Betrayal cuts deeply.

Not because of what was done—
But because of who did it.

Someone you trusted.
Someone you believed in.
Someone you did not expect to hurt you.

And those wounds can be difficult to release.

But even betrayal is not beyond God's healing.

He sees what happened.
He understands the pain.
And He is able to restore what was broken within you.

Prophetic Declaration

I declare that I am healed from every betrayal.

What was done to me will not define me.
I release the pain and refuse to live in offense.

God is restoring my heart
And making me whole again.

Prayer

Father, heal the places within me that were wounded by betrayal.

Help me to release the pain
And to trust You again.

Restore my heart fully.

In Jesus' name,
Amen.

Reflection Question

Am I still holding onto pain from someone who betrayed me?

Day 12

Emotional Restoration

Scripture (KJV)

"Create in me a clean heart, O God; and renew a right spirit within me."
— *Psalm 51:10*

Reflection

Emotional wounds are not always visible—
But they are real.

They affect how you respond,
How you trust,
How you connect with others.

And sometimes, you may not even realize how much has been affected.

But God is able to restore not just your spirit—
But your emotions.

He can bring balance where there has been instability.
Peace where there has been turmoil.

You do not have to remain overwhelmed.

Prophetic Declaration

I declare that my emotions are being restored.

I receive peace where there has been confusion.
I receive stability where there has been instability.

My heart is being renewed.
My spirit is being strengthened.

Prayer

Father, restore my emotions.

Where I have felt overwhelmed or unsettled,
Bring Your peace.

Renew my heart
And establish stability within me.

In Jesus' name,
Amen.

Reflection Question

In what areas do I need emotional healing and stability?

Day 13

Wholeness in Christ

Scripture (KJV)

"And ye are complete in him…"
— *Colossians 2:10*

Reflection

There is a difference between being healed…
And being whole.

Healing restores what was broken.
Wholeness establishes completeness.

Many people live as though something is missing—
As though they need something external to feel complete.

But your completeness is not found in people.
It is not found in circumstances.

It is found in Christ.

You are not lacking.
You are complete in Him.

Prophetic Declaration

I declare that I am whole in Christ.

Nothing is missing.
Nothing is broken.
Nothing is lacking in my life.

I am complete in Him
And I walk in that fullness daily.

Prayer

Father, thank You that I am complete in You.

Remove every mindset that makes me feel like I am lacking.

Help me to walk in wholeness
And to live from a place of completeness.

In Jesus' name,
Amen.

Reflection Question

Have I been looking to people or situations to make me feel complete?

Day 14

Peace Within

Scripture (KJV)

"And the peace of God, which passeth all understanding, shall keep your hearts and minds through Christ Jesus."
— *Philippians 4:7*

Reflection

Peace is not the absence of challenges.
It is the presence of God within you.

There may be things around you that are uncertain.
Situations that are unresolved.

But your peace does not come from everything being perfect—
It comes from trusting God.

There is a peace available to you
That is not dependent on circumstances.

A peace that guards your heart.
A peace that steadies your mind.
You do not have to live in anxiety.

You can live in peace.

Prophetic Declaration

I declare that I walk in the peace of God.

My heart is guarded.
My mind is stable.
My spirit is at rest.

I refuse anxiety, fear, and unrest.
I receive divine peace.

Prayer

Father, fill me with Your peace.

Where there has been anxiety or worry,
Let Your peace take over.

Guard my heart and mind
And keep me steady in You.

In Jesus' name, Amen.

Reflection Question

What is trying to disturb my peace—and how can I surrender it to God?

Week 2 Closing

You have completed Week 2.

You have released.
You have allowed healing to begin.

What once held you
Is losing its grip.

What once defined you
Is being replaced with truth.

You are not carrying the same weight.

You are becoming lighter.
Stronger.
Freer.

Prophetic Charge

I am healed.
I walk in freedom and wholeness.

Week 3

Faith —
Trusting God Completely

Anchor Scripture (KJV)

"For we walk by faith, not by sight."
— *2 Corinthians 5:7*

EXHORTATION

PART 1

Faith is not just something you have—
It is how you live.

It is possible to believe in God…
And still struggle to trust Him fully.

Because faith is tested most
When life does not make sense.

When prayers seem unanswered…
When timing feels delayed…
When circumstances look opposite of what you expected…

That is where faith is formed.

EXHORTATION

PART 2

Faith is not the absence of questions.
It is the decision to trust God anyway.

It is choosing to believe His Word
Even when your reality is saying something different.

It is standing firm
When everything around you feels uncertain.

Faith is not passive.
It is active.

It speaks.
It declares.
It holds on.

EXHORTATION

PART 3

This week, you will strengthen your trust in God.

Not based on feelings—
But based on truth.

You will learn to:

- Stand on His Word
- Trust His timing
- Overcome fear
- Speak with confidence

And as you do—
Your faith will become unshakable.

PROPHETIC PRAYER

Father, in the name of Jesus,

Strengthen my faith.

Where I have doubted, help me believe.
Where I have feared, help me trust.
Where I have questioned, bring clarity.

Teach me to rely on You completely.

Let my confidence be rooted in Your Word—
Not in circumstances.

I choose to trust You fully.

In Jesus' name,
Amen.

WEEKLY AFFIRMATION

I walk by faith and not by sight.
I trust God completely in every area
of my life.

Day 15

Walking by Faith

Scripture (KJV)

"For we walk by faith, not by sight."
— *2 Corinthians 5:7*

Reflection

Faith is not about what you see.
It is about what you believe.

If you only move based on what is visible,
You will always be limited.

But faith calls you higher.

It invites you to trust beyond evidence.
To move beyond comfort.
To believe beyond what is currently in front of you.

Walking by faith means
You are not controlled by circumstances.

You are led by truth.

Prophetic Declaration

I declare that I walk by faith and not by sight.

I am not controlled by what I see or feel.
I am led by the Word of God.

I trust God in every situation.
My steps are ordered by Him.

Prayer

Father, teach me to walk by faith.

Help me to trust You beyond what I can see
And to follow Your direction with confidence.

In Jesus' name,
Amen.

Reflection Question

Am I making decisions based on faith or based on what I see?

Day 16

Trusting God's Timing

Scripture (KJV)

"To every thing there is a season, and a time to every purpose under the heaven."
— *Ecclesiastes 3:1*

Reflection

Timing can be one of the hardest things to trust.

You may know what God has said…
But not understand when it will happen.

And in those moments,
It is easy to feel frustrated or discouraged.

But God is not late.
And He is not early.

He is precise.

What He has promised will come to pass—
At the right time.

Prophetic Declaration

I declare that I trust God's timing.

I will not rush ahead,
And I will not lose hope in waiting.

What God has spoken over my life will come to pass
At the appointed time.

Prayer

Father, help me to trust Your timing.

Remove impatience and frustration
And replace it with peace and confidence.

Teach me to wait with faith.

In Jesus' name,
Amen.

Reflection Question

Am I trusting God's timing, or am I trying to control it?

Day 17

Overcoming Fear

Scripture (KJV)

"For God hath not given us the spirit of fear; but of power, and of love, and of a sound mind."
— *2 Timothy 1:7*

Reflection

Fear is one of the greatest enemies of faith.

It speaks loudly.
It creates doubt.
It magnifies problems.

And if you listen to it long enough,
It will keep you from moving forward.

But fear is not from God.

You have been given power.
You have been given love.
You have been given a sound mind.

Fear does not define you.
Faith does.

Prophetic Declaration

I declare that I overcome every form of fear.

I walk in power, love, and a sound mind.
I refuse to be controlled by fear.

I choose faith over fear in every situation.

Prayer

Father, remove every fear from my life.

Help me to walk boldly in the authority You have given me
And to trust You fully.

In Jesus' name,
Amen.

Reflection Question

What fear has been holding me back from moving forward?

Day 18

Standing on God's Word

Scripture (KJV)

"Heaven and earth shall pass away: but my words shall not pass away."
— *Matthew 24:35*

Reflection

Everything around you can change.

Situations shift.
People change.
Circumstances rise and fall.

But one thing remains constant—
The Word of God.

When you stand on His Word,
You are standing on something unshakable.

Not emotions.
Not opinions.
Not temporary outcomes.

But truth.

And truth does not fail.

Prophetic Declaration

I declare that I stand firmly on the Word of God.

His Word is my foundation.
His Word is my truth.
His Word is unchanging.

No matter what I face,
I remain grounded in what God has said.

Prayer

Father, help me to stand on Your Word.

When everything feels uncertain,
Let Your truth be my anchor.

Strengthen my faith in Your promises.

In Jesus' name,
Amen.

Reflection Question

Am I standing on God's Word—or on my emotions and circumstances?

Day 19

Faith Over Feelings

Scripture (KJV)

"For we live by faith, not by sight."
— *2 Corinthians 5:7*

Reflection

Feelings are real—
But they are not always reliable.

They change.
They shift.
They respond to circumstances.

But faith is different.

Faith is rooted in truth, not emotion.

There will be days you do not feel strong.
Days you do not feel confident.
Days you do not feel hopeful.

But those feelings do not define your reality.

Truth does.

Prophetic Declaration

I declare that I live by faith, not by feelings.

My emotions do not control me.
The Word of God leads me.

Even when I do not feel it,
I choose to believe it.

Prayer

Father, help me to rise above my emotions.

Teach me to trust Your Word
More than what I feel.

Establish my faith in truth.

In Jesus' name,
Amen.

Reflection Question

Do my feelings lead my decisions, or does my faith?

Day 20

Confidence in God

Scripture (KJV)

"Being confident of this very thing, that he which hath begun a good work in you will perform it…"
— *Philippians 1:6*

Reflection

Confidence is not arrogance.

It is assurance.

Not in yourself alone—
But in God working through you.

God does not start what He cannot finish.

If He began something in your life,
He is committed to completing it.

You do not have to question the process.
You do not have to doubt the outcome.

Your confidence is not in your ability—
It is in His faithfulness.

Prophetic Declaration

I declare that I am confident in God.

What He started in my life, He will complete.
I do not doubt His process.
I trust His faithfulness.

I walk with boldness and assurance.

Prayer

Father, strengthen my confidence in You.

Help me to trust that what You have started
Will be completed.

Remove every doubt
And establish bold faith within me.

In Jesus' name,
Amen.

Reflection Question

Where in my life do I need to trust that God will finish what He started?

Day 21

Unshakable Faith

Scripture (KJV)

"Jesus said unto him, If thou canst believe, all things are possible to him that believeth."
— *Mark 9:23*

Reflection

Faith grows.

It starts small—
But it becomes strong through consistency.

Through choosing to believe again and again…
Through standing even when it is difficult…
Through trusting God in every season…

Faith becomes unshakable.

Not because life is easy—
But because your trust is firm.

There will always be challenges.
But they will no longer move you.

Because your faith is rooted.

Prophetic Declaration

I declare that my faith is unshakable.

I believe God in all things.
I trust Him in every season.

Nothing will move me.
Nothing will break my confidence.

I stand firm in faith.

Prayer

Father, establish unshakable faith within me.

Help me to trust You completely
No matter what I face.

Let my faith grow stronger every day.

In Jesus' name,
Amen.

Reflection Question

What would my life look like if my faith was truly unshakable?

Week 3 Closing

You have completed Week 3.

Your faith has been strengthened.

Not just in what you say—
But in what you believe.

You now stand differently.

With trust.
With confidence.
With clarity.

Faith is no longer a concept.

It is your lifestyle.

Prophetic Charge

I walk by faith.
I trust God completely.

Week 4

Purpose — Walking in Divine Assignment

Anchor Scripture (KJV)

"For we are his workmanship, created in Christ Jesus unto good works, which God hath before ordained that we should walk in them."

— *Ephesians 2:10*

EXHORTATION

PART 1

You were not created randomly.

Your life is intentional.
Your existence is purposeful.
Your journey is designed.

There is something God placed within you—
A calling, an assignment, a divine purpose.

And whether you have fully discovered it yet or not…
It is there.

EXHORTATION

PART 2

Many people spend their lives searching for purpose
As though it is something far away.

But purpose is not distant.
It is revealed as you walk with God.

It unfolds in obedience.
It becomes clear in movement.

You do not have to have everything figured out—
You just have to take the next step.

EXHORTATION

PART 3

This week is about alignment.

Aligning your life with what God has already written.
Aligning your steps with His direction.
Aligning your voice with your assignment.

You are not called to watch life happen—
You are called to walk in purpose.

And as you begin to move—
Clarity will come.

WEEKLY PROPHETIC PRAYER

Father, in the name of Jesus,

I thank You for the purpose You have placed upon my life.

Open my eyes to see clearly.
Direct my steps.
Align my heart with Your will.

Remove confusion and hesitation.
Give me boldness to walk in what You have called me to do.

Let my life reflect Your intention.

In Jesus' name,
Amen.

WEEKLY AFFIRMATION

I am walking in purpose.
My life is aligned with God's divine plan.

Day 22

Called for a Purpose

Scripture (KJV)

"Many are called, but few are chosen."
— *Matthew 22:14*

Reflection

You are not here by accident.

Your life carries meaning.
Your existence carries purpose.

God did not create you to simply exist—
He created you to fulfill something.

There is a call on your life.

And that call is not reserved for a few—
It includes you.

Prophetic Declaration

I declare that I am called for a purpose.

My life is not empty.
My life is not random.

I carry divine assignment
And I walk in it boldly.

Prayer

Father, thank You for calling me.

Help me to recognize and embrace
The purpose You have placed on my life.

In Jesus' name,
Amen.

Reflection Question

Do I believe that my life has a specific purpose?

Day 23

Equipped by God

Scripture (KJV)

"I can do all things through Christ which strengtheneth me."
— *Philippians 4:13*

Reflection

Sometimes, the greatest barrier to purpose
Is not opportunity—it is doubt.

You may feel unqualified.
Unprepared.
Not ready.

But God does not call the equipped—
He equips the called.

Everything you need to fulfill your purpose
Has already been made available to you through Him.

You are not lacking.
You are equipped.

Prophetic Declaration

I declare that I am equipped by God.

I have everything I need
To fulfill my purpose.

I do not walk in limitation—
I walk in divine ability.

Prayer

Father, help me to trust
That I am equipped for what You have called me to do.

Remove every doubt
And strengthen my confidence in You.

In Jesus' name,
Amen.

Reflection Question

Where have I doubted my ability to fulfill what God has called me to do?

Day 24

Walking in Obedience

Scripture (KJV)

"And Samuel said, Hath the Lord as great delight in burnt offerings and sacrifices, as in obeying the voice of the Lord?"
— *1 Samuel 15:22*

Reflection

Purpose is not just discovered—
It is walked out through obedience.

God may not show you everything at once.
But He will always show you the next step.

And often, clarity comes after obedience.

Not before.

Obedience may not always feel comfortable.
But it will always lead you into alignment.

Prophetic Declaration

I declare that I walk in obedience.

I respond to God's voice with willingness.
I do not delay or resist.

My steps are aligned with His direction.

Prayer

Father, help me to obey You fully.

Give me the courage
To follow Your direction without hesitation.

In Jesus' name,
Amen.

Reflection Question

Is there something God has asked me to do that I have delayed?

Day 25

Boldness in Calling

Scripture (KJV)

"And they were all filled with the Holy Ghost, and they spake the word of God with boldness."
— *Acts 4:31*

Reflection

Purpose requires boldness.

Not loudness.
Not perfection.
But courage.

There will be moments when you feel unsure.
Moments when you question yourself.

But boldness is not the absence of fear—
It is the decision to move forward anyway.

You were not called to hide what God placed inside of you.
You were called to walk in it—boldly.

Prophetic Declaration

I declare that I walk in boldness.

I do not shrink back.
I do not hide my calling.

I step forward with confidence
And fulfill what God has placed on my life.

Prayer

Father, give me boldness.

Help me to move forward
Without fear or hesitation.

Strengthen me to walk fully
In my calling.

In Jesus' name,
Amen.

Reflection Question

Where in my life do I need to step out with boldness?

Day 26

Faithfulness in Small Things

Scripture (KJV)

"He that is faithful in that which is least is faithful also in much…"
— *Luke 16:10*

Reflection

Purpose is not only revealed in big moments—
It is built in small ones.

The daily decisions.
The unseen efforts.
The consistent actions.

It is easy to desire something greater—
But greatness is prepared in the small.

What you do consistently matters.

God sees what others do not see.
And He honors faithfulness.

Prophetic Declaration

I declare that I am faithful in all things.

I do not despise small beginnings.
I remain consistent and committed.

What I do daily is preparing me
For what is ahead.

Prayer

Father, help me to be faithful.

Even in the small things,
Help me to remain consistent and committed.

Prepare me for what You have ahead.

In Jesus' name,
Amen.

Reflection Question

Am I being faithful in the small things God has placed before me?

Day 27

Impacting Lives

Scripture (KJV)

"Let your light so shine before men, that they may see your good works…"
— *Matthew 5:16*

Reflection

Your life is not just for you.

There are people connected to your purpose.
Lives that will be touched by your obedience.
Hearts that will be changed through what you carry.

You may not always see the impact immediately—
But it is there.

When you walk in purpose,
You naturally affect others.

Your life carries influence.

Prophetic Declaration

I declare that my life makes an impact.

My actions, my words, and my obedience
Are touching lives.

I shine the light of God
In everything I do.

Prayer

Father, use my life.

Let everything I do
Reflect You.

Help me to walk in purpose
In a way that impacts others.

In Jesus' name,
Amen.

Reflection Question

How can I intentionally allow my life to impact others?

Day 28

Living Intentionally

Scripture (KJV)

"See then that ye walk circumspectly, not as fools, but as wise."
— *Ephesians 5:15*

Reflection

Purpose requires intention.

It is not something you drift into—
It is something you choose daily.

How you think.
How you speak.
How you act.

Every decision matters.

Living intentionally means
You are aware of how you are living
And aligned with why you are living.

You are no longer just reacting—
You are choosing.

Prophetic Declaration

I declare that I live intentionally.

My life is aligned with purpose.
My decisions are guided by wisdom.

I do not live randomly—
I live with direction and clarity.

Prayer

Father, help me to live intentionally.

Guide my thoughts, my actions, and my decisions.

Let my life reflect purpose
In everything I do.

In Jesus' name,
Amen.

Reflection Question

Am I living intentionally—or just going through life without direction?

WEEK 4 CLOSING

You have completed Week 4.

Purpose is no longer something you are searching for—
It is something you are stepping into.

You have begun to move.
To respond.
To align.

What once felt distant
Is now becoming clear.

You are not here by accident.
You are walking in divine assignment.

And as you continue—
Your steps will become more confident,
Your direction more defined,
And your impact more visible.

Because when purpose is embraced—
Life gains direction.

Prophetic Charge

I walk in purpose.
My life is aligned with God's plan.

Week 5

Strength — Standing Firm in All Seasons

Anchor Scripture (KJV)

"I can do all things through Christ which strengtheneth me."
— *Philippians 4:13*

EXHORTATION

PART 1

Strength is not just physical.

It is spiritual.
It is emotional.
It is mental.

Life will present moments that test you.
Moments that stretch you.
Moments that require more from you than you feel you have.

And in those moments,
You will need strength.

EXHORTATION

PART 2

But your strength is not limited to you.

God does not expect you to carry life on your own.

His strength is made available to you.

In weakness—He strengthens.
In pressure—He sustains.
In difficulty—He upholds.

You are not alone in what you are facing.

EXHORTATION

PART 3

This week is about standing.

Standing when things are uncertain.
Standing when things are difficult.
Standing when you feel tired.

Not because you have all the answers—
But because your strength comes from God.

And as you stand—
You will not break.

You will become stronger.

WEEKLY PROPHETIC PRAYER

Father, in the name of Jesus,

Strengthen me.

In every area where I feel weak,
Be my strength.

When I feel overwhelmed, sustain me.
When I feel tired, renew me.
When I feel uncertain, stabilize me.

I do not rely on myself—
I rely on You.

In Jesus' name,
Amen.

WEEKLY AFFIRMATION

I am strong in the Lord.
I stand firm in every season.

Day 29

Strength in Weakness

Scripture (KJV)

"My grace is sufficient for thee: for my strength is made perfect in weakness…"
— *2 Corinthians 12:9*

Reflection

Weakness is not failure.

It is often the place
Where God's strength becomes most visible.

There are moments when you feel like you cannot continue.
Like you have reached your limit.

But God meets you there.

Not when you are strong on your own—
But when you recognize your need for Him.

Your weakness is not your end.
It is the place where strength begins.

Prophetic Declaration

I declare that God's strength is perfected in me.

In every place of weakness,
I receive His strength.

I am not defeated—
I am strengthened.

Prayer

Father, in my weakness, be my strength.

Help me to rely on You
And not on my own ability.

Strengthen me in every area of my life.

In Jesus' name,
Amen.

Reflection Question

Where do I feel weak—and how can I allow God to strengthen me in that area?

Day 30

Endurance

Scripture (KJV)

"But they that wait upon the Lord shall renew their strength…"
— *Isaiah 40:31*

Reflection

Endurance is the ability to continue
Even when things are not easy.

It is not about speed—
It is about consistency.

There will be seasons that feel long.
Moments that feel stretched.

But endurance keeps you moving.

And when your strength feels low—
God renews it.

You are not running alone.
You are being sustained.

Prophetic Declaration

I declare that I endure with strength.

I do not give up.
I do not quit.

God renews my strength daily,
And I continue forward.

Prayer

Father, help me to endure.

When I feel tired or discouraged,
Renew my strength.

Help me to continue
With faith and perseverance.

In Jesus' name,
Amen.

Reflection Question

Where in my life do I need endurance right now?

Day 31

Not Growing Weary

Scripture (KJV)

"And let us not be weary in well doing…"
— *Galatians 6:9*

Reflection

Doing the right thing
Does not always feel easy.

There are times when you give,
Serve,
Show up—
And feel tired.

But weariness does not mean you should stop.

It means you need renewal.

You are not wasting your efforts.
You are not unseen.

There is a reward for consistency.

Prophetic Declaration

I declare that I will not grow weary.

I remain strong in doing what is right.
I stay consistent and committed.

My efforts are not in vain.

Prayer

Father, strengthen me
So I do not grow weary.

Renew my energy and my focus.

Help me to continue faithfully.

In Jesus' name,
Amen.

Reflection Question

Where have I felt like giving up—and why?

Day 32

Renewed Strength

Scripture (KJV)

"But they that wait upon the Lord shall renew their strength…"
— *Isaiah 40:31*

Reflection

Strength is not just something you have—
It is something that can be renewed.

There are moments when you feel drained.
When life has taken more than you expected.

But God does not leave you empty.

As you wait on Him—
Not in frustration, but in trust—
He renews what has been depleted.

You do not have to remain exhausted.
There is renewal available to you.

Prophetic Declaration

I declare that my strength is being renewed.

I am not depleted.
I am refreshed.

God is restoring my energy,
My focus, and my capacity.

Prayer

Father, renew my strength.

Where I feel drained,
Fill me again.

Restore every part of me
That has been worn down.

In Jesus' name,
Amen.

Reflection Question

Where do I need renewal in my life right now?

Day 33

Stability in God

Scripture (KJV)

"Thou wilt keep him in perfect peace, whose mind is stayed on thee…"
— *Isaiah 26:3*

Reflection

Stability is not found in circumstances—
It is found in God.

Life can be unpredictable.
Situations can change quickly.

But when your mind is fixed on God,
You remain steady.

You are not shaken by every change.
You are not moved by every situation.

You are anchored.

Prophetic Declaration

I declare that I am stable in God.

My mind is fixed on Him.
My heart is at peace.

I am not shaken.
I am grounded and steady.

Prayer

Father, establish stability within me.

Help me to keep my focus on You
And not on what is changing around me.

Let Your peace anchor me.

In Jesus' name,
Amen.

Reflection Question

What has been affecting my stability—and how can I refocus on God?

Day 34

Standing Firm

Scripture (KJV)

"Stand fast therefore in the liberty wherewith Christ hath made us free…"
— *Galatians 5:1*

Reflection

Standing firm means you do not move easily.

Not because life is easy—
But because you are grounded.

There will always be pressure.
There will always be challenges.

But you are not called to be easily shaken.

You are called to stand.

Firm in truth.
Firm in faith.
Firm in identity.

Prophetic Declaration

I declare that I stand firm.

I am not easily shaken.
I am not easily moved.

I remain grounded in truth
And steady in every season.

Prayer

Father, help me to stand firm.

When pressure comes,
Strengthen me.

Let me remain steady
In every situation.

In Jesus' name,
Amen.

Reflection Question

Where do I need to stand firm instead of giving in?

Day 35

Strength Through God

Scripture (KJV)

"The Lord is my strength and my shield…"
— *Psalm 28:7*

Reflection

True strength does not come from within alone—
It comes from God.

You are not meant to rely solely on yourself.

When you depend on God,
You access a strength that does not fail.

A strength that sustains you.
A strength that carries you.
A strength that protects you.

You are not weak—
You are supported.

Prophetic Declaration

I declare that God is my strength.

I do not rely on myself alone.
I am sustained by Him.

I am strong,
Because He strengthens me.

Prayer

Father, be my strength.

Help me to depend on You fully
And to trust in Your power.

Strengthen me in every area of my life.

In Jesus' name,
Amen.

Reflection Question

Am I relying on my own strength—or on God's?

WEEK 5 CLOSING

You have completed Week 5.

You have learned to stand.

Not in your own strength—
But in God's strength.

You have endured.
You have remained.
You have been strengthened.

You are no longer easily shaken.

There is stability within you.
There is strength within you.

And as you continue—
You will face life differently.

Not with fear…but with confidence.

Because when strength is established—
You do not break under pressure.

You stand.

Prophetic Charge

I am strong in the Lord.
I stand firm in every season.

Week 6

Relationships - Godly Connections

Anchor Scripture (KJV)

"Be not deceived: evil communications corrupt good manners."
— *1 Corinthians 15:33*

EXHORTATION

PART 1

Relationships matter.

The people around you influence you—
Your thinking, your decisions, your direction.

Some relationships build you.
Some drain you.
Some shape you in ways you may not immediately notice.

And whether you realize it or not…
Who you are connected to matters.

EXHORTATION

PART 2

Not every connection is meant to remain.

Some people are assigned to your life for a season.
Some for a purpose.
Some for growth.

And some… you must release.

Discernment is necessary.

You do not have to hold onto what is no longer aligned.
And you do not have to force what God is not sustaining.

EXHORTATION

PART 3

Godly relationships bring peace.
Clarity.
Growth.

They do not confuse you.
They do not pull you away from your purpose.
They do not drain your strength.

This week is about alignment.

Who is in your life.
Who should remain.
Who should not.

And how you position yourself in relationships.

WEEKLY PROPHETIC PRAYER

Father, in the name of Jesus,

Align my relationships.

Bring the right people into my life.
Strengthen the connections that are from You.
And give me wisdom to release what is not.

Give me discernment.
Help me to recognize what is healthy
And what is not.

Let my relationships reflect Your will.

In Jesus' name,
Amen.

WEEKLY AFFIRMATION

My relationships are aligned with God.

I am surrounded by the right people.

Day 36

Godly Connections

Scripture (KJV)

"Two are better than one…"
— *Ecclesiastes 4:9*

Reflection

Not every connection is beneficial.

But Godly connections add value.

They support you.
Encourage you.
Strengthen you.

They do not compete with you—
They complement you.

God brings people into your life
Who are aligned with your purpose.

You are not meant to walk alone.

Prophetic Declaration

I declare that I am connected to the right people.

My relationships are aligned with my purpose.
I am surrounded by those who build me up
And not tear me down.

Prayer

Father, bring the right people into my life.

Help me to recognize and value
Godly connections.

Strengthen every relationship that is from You.

In Jesus' name,
Amen.

Reflection Question

Are my current relationships helping me grow or holding me back?

Day 37

Discernment in Relationships

Scripture (KJV)

"Beloved, believe not every spirit, but try the spirits whether they are of God…"
— *1 John 4:1*

Reflection

Not everyone who comes into your life
Is meant to stay.

And not everything that looks good
Is good.

Discernment helps you see beyond appearances.

It helps you recognize intention.
It helps you avoid unnecessary pain.

You do not have to accept every connection.
You have the wisdom to choose.

Prophetic Declaration

I declare that I walk in discernment.

I see clearly.
I recognize what is from God
And what is not.

I make wise decisions in my relationships.

Prayer

Father, give me discernment.

Help me to see clearly
And to make wise decisions in my relationships.

Protect me from wrong connections.

In Jesus' name,
Amen.

Reflection Question

Have I ignored signs in relationships that I should have paid attention to?

Day 38

Setting Boundaries

Scripture (KJV)

"Keep thy heart with all diligence; for out of it are the issues of life."
— *Proverbs 4:23*

Reflection

Boundaries are not rejection.

They are protection.

You are responsible for your peace.
For your energy.
For your emotional and spiritual well-being.

Not everyone should have full access to you.

And that is okay.

Healthy boundaries create healthy relationships.

Prophetic Declaration

I declare that I set healthy boundaries.

I protect my peace.
I guard my heart.
I do not allow anything that disturbs my alignment.

Prayer

Father, teach me to set boundaries.

Help me to protect what You have given me
Without guilt or fear.

In Jesus' name,
Amen.

Reflection Question

Where do I need to establish stronger boundaries?

Day 39

Avoiding Toxic Relationships

Scripture (KJV)

"Make no friendship with an angry man; and with a furious man thou shalt not go."
— *Proverbs 22:24*

Reflection

Not every relationship is healthy.

Some relationships drain you.
Confuse you.
Pull you away from who you are meant to be.

And sometimes, it is not obvious at first.

But over time, the effect becomes clear.

You are not called to remain in environments
That weaken you.

Wisdom knows when to step back.

Prophetic Declaration

I declare that I walk away from toxic relationships.

I do not remain where I am drained, confused, or weakened.

I choose peace.
I choose clarity.
I choose what is healthy.

Prayer

Father, give me the wisdom
To recognize unhealthy relationships.

Help me to step away from what is not good for me
And to walk in peace.

In Jesus' name,
Amen.

Reflection Question

Is there a relationship in my life that is negatively affecting me?

Day 40

Walking in Love and Wisdom

Scripture (KJV)

"Let all your things be done with charity."
— *1 Corinthians 16:14*

Reflection

Love is essential in every relationship.

But love must be balanced with wisdom.

You can love people
Without allowing them to misuse you.

You can care deeply
Without losing yourself.

Love does not mean
You ignore what is unhealthy.

It means you respond with grace
While still walking in truth.

Prophetic Declaration

I declare that I walk in love and wisdom.

I love genuinely,
But I also walk with understanding.

I do not lose myself in relationships.
I remain aligned and grounded.

Prayer

Father, help me to walk in love.

Give me the wisdom
To love in a healthy and balanced way.

In Jesus' name,
Amen.

Reflection Question

Am I balancing love with wisdom in my relationships?

Day 41

Forgiveness in Relationships

Scripture (KJV)

"Forbearing one another, and forgiving one another…"
— *Colossians 3:13*

Reflection

No relationship is perfect.

People will make mistakes.
They will say things they should not say.
They will sometimes hurt you.

And if you hold onto that hurt,
It begins to affect you more than it affects them.

Forgiveness is not excusing what happened.
It is releasing its hold on you.

You do not forgive because they deserve it—
You forgive because you deserve peace.

Prophetic Declaration

I declare that I walk in forgiveness.

I release every offense.
I let go of every hurt.

I choose peace over resentment.
I choose freedom over bitterness.

Prayer

Father, help me to forgive.

Remove every bitterness from my heart.
Help me to release what I have been holding onto.

In Jesus' name,
Amen.

Reflection Question

Is there someone I need to forgive?

Day 42

Healthy Connections

Scripture (KJV)

"Iron sharpeneth iron; so a man sharpeneth the countenance of his friend."
— *Proverbs 27:17*

Reflection

Healthy relationships sharpen you.

They challenge you.
They strengthen you.
They encourage growth.

They do not leave you the same—
They help you become better.

You should be able to grow in your relationships,
Not shrink.

You should feel strengthened,
Not diminished.

Godly connections refine you.

Prophetic Declaration

I declare that I have healthy connections.

My relationships strengthen me.
They sharpen me.
They help me grow.

I am surrounded by people
Who add value to my life.

Prayer

Father, establish healthy relationships in my life.

Remove what is not aligned
And strengthen what is.

Let my connections reflect growth and purpose.

In Jesus' name,
Amen.

Reflection Question

Do my relationships sharpen me or weaken me?

WEEK 6 CLOSING

You have completed Week 6.

You now see relationships differently.

With clarity.
With wisdom.
With discernment.

You understand that not every connection is meant to remain.
And not every relationship is meant to shape your life.

You have learned to:
Discern,
Set boundaries,
Walk in love,
And choose what is healthy.

And as you continue—
Your relationships will begin to reflect alignment.

Because when your connections are right—
Your life flows differently.

Prophetic Charge

My relationships are aligned.
I am connected to what is right for me.

Week 7:

Marriage & Family — Building Godly Foundations

Anchor Scripture (KJV)

"Except the Lord build the house, they labour in vain that build it…"
— *Psalm 127:1*

EXHORTATION

PART 1

Family is not just a structure.
It is a foundation.

It shapes identity.
It influences direction.
It impacts generations.

Whether through marriage, children, or future desires—
Family is deeply significant.

And because of that, it must be built intentionally.

EXHORTATION

PART 2

Marriage and family are not sustained by effort alone.

They require wisdom.
They require patience.
They require alignment with God.

There will be moments of joy.
Moments of growth.
And moments that require grace.

But when God is at the center—
Strength is established.

EXHORTATION

PART 3

This week is for every woman.

For the married—
For the single—
For the one preparing—
For the one healing—

God's design for family is still good.

And your story is still being written.

WEEKLY PROPHETIC PRAYER

Father, in the name of Jesus,

I commit my family into Your hands.

Where there is healing needed—bring restoration.
Where there is confusion—bring clarity.
Where there is distance—bring unity.

Establish Your presence in my home.
Guide my role, my words, and my actions.

Let my family reflect Your peace and purpose.

In Jesus' name,
Amen.

WEEKLY AFFIRMATION

My family is established in God.
My home is filled with peace,
wisdom, and love.

Day 43

God at the Center

Scripture (KJV)

"Except the Lord build the house, they labour in vain that build it…"
— *Psalm 127:1*

Reflection

Everything begins with foundation.

If God is not at the center,
Everything else becomes difficult to sustain.

A home built on emotions alone will shake.
A relationship built on convenience will weaken.

But when God is at the center—
There is stability.

You are not responsible to carry everything.
God is.

Prophetic Declaration

I declare that God is at the center of my life and my home.

Everything I build is established in Him.
My relationships are strengthened by His presence.

Prayer

Father, be at the center of my life.

Guide my home, my relationships,
And everything connected to me.

In Jesus' name,
Amen.

Reflection Question

Is God truly at the center of my life and relationships?

Day 44

Peace in the Home

Scripture (KJV)

"And let the peace of God rule in your hearts…"
— *Colossians 3:15*

Reflection

Peace is essential in a home.

Not perfection—
Peace.

There may be differences.
Different personalities.
Different perspectives.

But peace brings balance.

It creates an environment
Where love can grow
And where hearts can rest.

You have the ability to carry peace.

Prophetic Declaration

I declare that my home is filled with peace.

I do not bring confusion—
I bring calmness.

God's peace rules in my home.

Prayer

Father, establish peace in my home.

Remove every form of tension
And replace it with calmness and understanding.

In Jesus' name,
Amen.

Reflection Question

What can I do to bring more peace into my home?

Day 45

Wisdom in Relationships

Scripture (KJV)

"Through wisdom is an house builded; and by understanding it is established."
— *Proverbs 24:3*

Reflection

Love alone is not enough.

Wisdom builds.
Understanding sustains.

In relationships,
It is not just what you feel—
It is how you respond.

Wisdom helps you:

- Speak carefully
- Respond correctly
- Handle situations with maturity

A strong home is built through wisdom.

Prophetic Declaration

I declare that I walk in wisdom.

My words are guided.
My actions are intentional.

I build my relationships with understanding.

Prayer

Father, give me wisdom.

Help me to respond with understanding
And to build my relationships the right way.

In Jesus' name,
Amen.

Reflection Question

Do I respond in my relationships with wisdom or with emotion?

Day 46

Love and Respect

Scripture (KJV)

"Let all your things be done with charity."
— *1 Corinthians 16:14*

Reflection

Love is the foundation of every relationship.

But love must be expressed—
Through words,
Through actions,
Through attitude.

Respect strengthens love.

It creates an environment
Where people feel valued,
Heard,
And understood.

In every relationship,
How you treat others matters.

Love and respect build what emotions alone cannot sustain.

Prophetic Declaration

I declare that I walk in love and respect.

My words are kind.
My actions reflect grace.

I build my relationships through love and honor.

Prayer

Father, help me to walk in love.

Teach me to treat others with respect
And to build healthy relationships.

In Jesus' name,
Amen.

Reflection Question

Do my words and actions reflect love and respect?

Day 47

Healing in the Family

Scripture (KJV)

"He healeth the broken in heart, and bindeth up their wounds."
— *Psalm 147:3*

Reflection

Not every family is perfect.

There may be wounds.
Misunderstandings.
Moments that left pain.

But healing is possible.

God is able to restore
Even what feels broken.

It may take time.
It may require patience.

But restoration begins
When healing is allowed.

Prophetic Declaration

I declare that healing is taking place in my family.

Every broken place is being restored.
Every wound is being healed.

Peace is returning.
Wholeness is being established.

Prayer

Father, bring healing to my family.

Restore every broken relationship.
Heal every place that has been hurt.

In Jesus' name,
Amen.

Reflection Question

What area of my family needs healing right now?

Day 48

Unity in the Home

Scripture (KJV)

"Behold, how good and how pleasant it is for brethren to dwell together in unity!"
— *Psalm 133:1*

Reflection

Unity does not mean everyone is the same.

It means there is agreement,
Peace,
And understanding.

A divided home struggles.
A united home stands strong.

Unity requires effort.
It requires humility.
It requires choosing peace over pride.

When unity is present,
Strength increases.

Prophetic Declaration

I declare that there is unity in my home.

We walk in agreement.
We choose peace.
We build together.

My home is strong and united.

Prayer

Father, establish unity in my home.

Remove division and misunderstanding.
Help us to walk in peace and agreement.

In Jesus' name,
Amen.

Reflection Question

Am I contributing to unity or to division in my home?

Day 49

Strength in the Home

Scripture (KJV)

"God is our refuge and strength, a very present help in trouble."
— *Psalm 46:1*

Reflection

Every home faces challenges.

Moments of pressure.
Moments of uncertainty.

But strength is not found in avoiding difficulty—
It is found in facing it with God.

A strong home is not a perfect home.
It is a home that relies on God.

When God is your strength,
You do not break under pressure.

You stand.

Prophetic Declaration

I declare that my home is strong.

We are not shaken by challenges.
We are supported by God.

My home stands firm in every season.

Prayer

Father, be the strength of my home.

Help us to rely on You
In every situation.

Establish strength within our family.

In Jesus' name,
Amen.

Reflection Question

Where does my home need strength right now?

WEEK 7 CLOSING

You have completed Week 7.

You have spoken over your home.
Over your relationships.
Over your family.

You have chosen love.
You have chosen wisdom.
You have chosen peace.

And as you continue—
Your home will begin to reflect
What you have declared.

Because what is spoken consistently
Becomes established.

Your family is not left to chance.
It is being built intentionally.

Prophetic Charge

My home is established in God.
My family walks in peace, love, and unity.

Week 8:

Children & Legacy — Speaking Over the Next Generation

Anchor Scripture (KJV)

"And all thy children shall be taught of the Lord; and great shall be the peace of thy children."

— *Isaiah 54:13*

EXHORTATION

PART 1

Children are not just a part of your life—
They are a continuation of it.

Whether present now or in the future,
They carry purpose.

They carry identity.
They carry destiny.

And what is spoken over them matters.

EXHORTATION

PART 2

Words shape direction.

What you declare over your children
Becomes a covering.

A foundation.
A guide.

Even before you see results—
Your words are working.

This is not just about parenting.
It is about **stewardship of destiny**.

EXHORTATION

PART 3

This week is for:

The mother—
The future mother—
The spiritual mother—
The woman preparing—

You are not just raising children.
You are shaping a generation.

And your voice matters.

WEEKLY PROPHETIC PRAYER

Father, in the name of Jesus,

I commit my children and future generations into Your hands.

Cover them.
Guide them.
Protect them.

Let their lives be aligned with Your purpose.
Let their paths be directed by You.

I declare peace, wisdom, and destiny over them.

In Jesus' name,
Amen.

WEEKLY AFFIRMATION

My children are covered by God. Their lives are aligned with His purpose.

Day 50

Children Are a Blessing

Scripture (KJV)

"Lo, children are an heritage of the Lord…"
— *Psalm 127:3*

Reflection

Children are not a burden.
They are a blessing.

A gift.
A trust.
A responsibility given by God.

Even in challenging moments,
Their value does not change.

They are precious.
And they carry purpose.

Prophetic Declaration

I declare that children are a blessing.

They are a gift from God.
They are valuable and purposeful.

I receive them with gratitude and wisdom.

Prayer

Father, thank You for the gift of children.

Help me to value, guide, and nurture them
According to Your will.

In Jesus' name,
Amen.

Reflection Question

Do I truly see children as a blessing?

Day 51

Speaking Life Over Children

Scripture (KJV)

"Death and life are in the power of the tongue…"
— *Proverbs 18:21*

Reflection

Words matter.

Especially when spoken over children.

They are forming identity.
Building confidence.
Shaping belief.

Your words can strengthen—
Or weaken.

Speak life.
Speak purpose.
Speak truth.

Even when correction is needed—
Let it be covered with life.

Prophetic Declaration

I declare that I speak life over children.

My words build.
My words strengthen.
My words align with God's truth.

I speak destiny and purpose.

Prayer

Father, guide my words.

Help me to speak life,
Encouragement, and truth.

Let my voice build and not break.

In Jesus' name,
Amen.

Reflection Question

Are my words building or discouraging?

Day 52

Protection Over Children

Scripture (KJV)

"The Lord shall preserve thy going out and thy coming in…"
— *Psalm 121:8*

Reflection

Children need covering.

Not just physically—
But spiritually.

There are things you cannot control.
But there is a God who protects.

When you pray,
When you declare—
You are creating a covering.

They are not exposed.
They are protected.

Prophetic Declaration

I declare divine protection over children.

They are covered.
They are preserved.
They are safe.

God watches over them at all times.

Prayer

Father, protect every child.

Guard their lives,
Their paths,
And their future.

In Jesus' name,
Amen.

Reflection Question

Do I actively pray and declare protection over children?

Day 53

Wisdom and Guidance for Children

Scripture (KJV)

"If any of you lack wisdom, let him ask of God…"
—*James 1:5*

Reflection

Children need guidance.

Not just instruction—
But wisdom.

Life presents choices.
Directions.
Decisions.

And without guidance,
It is easy to go in the wrong direction.

But God gives wisdom freely.

As you pray and declare,
You are inviting divine direction into their lives.

Prophetic Declaration

I declare that children walk in wisdom.

Their decisions are guided by God.
Their paths are directed with clarity.

They do not walk in confusion—
They walk in understanding.

Prayer

Father, grant wisdom to every child.

Guide their decisions.
Direct their paths.

Let them walk in understanding.

In Jesus' name,
Amen.

Reflection Question

Am I intentionally praying for wisdom over children?

Day 54

Future and Destiny

Scripture (KJV)

"For I know the thoughts that I think toward you, saith the Lord…"
— *Jeremiah 29:11*

Reflection

Every child carries a future.

A purpose.
A calling.
A destiny.

What you see today
Is not the final picture.

There is more ahead.

And your declarations
Help align them with that future.

Do not limit them
By what you see now.

Speak into who they are becoming.

Prophetic Declaration

I declare that children walk in their destiny.

Their future is secure.
Their purpose is clear.

They become everything God has called them to be.

Prayer

Father, align every child with their destiny.

Guide their future
And establish their purpose.

In Jesus' name,
Amen.

Reflection Question

Do I speak into the future—or only focus on the present?

Day 55

Future Spouses

Scripture (KJV)

"Every good gift and every perfect gift is from above…"
— *James 1:17*

Reflection

The future matters.

Even the relationships your children will one day enter.

Marriage is not random.
It is a connection that shapes life.

And even now—
You can pray.

You can declare.

You can speak alignment
Over their future relationships.

God prepares both sides.

Prophetic Declaration

I declare that children are aligned with godly relationships.

Their future spouses are prepared by God.
Their relationships are healthy, strong, and purposeful.

They do not walk into confusion—
They walk into alignment.

Prayer

Father, prepare their future relationships.

Align them with the right people.
Guide their choices.

In Jesus' name,
Amen.

Reflection Question

Am I praying for the future relationships of children?

Day 56

Education and Growth

Scripture (KJV)

"And Jesus increased in wisdom and stature…"
— *Luke 2:52*

Reflection

Growth is intentional.

Learning.
Understanding.
Development.

Children are meant to grow—
Not just physically,
But mentally and spiritually.

Education is not just about knowledge—
It is about development.

You can speak growth.
You can declare progress.

Prophetic Declaration

I declare that children grow in wisdom and knowledge.

They excel in learning.
They develop in understanding.

They increase in every area of their lives.

Prayer

Father, bless their growth.

Help them to learn, develop, and increase
In every area.

In Jesus' name,
Amen.

Reflection Question

Am I actively speaking growth and progress over children?

WEEK 8 CLOSING

You have completed Week 8.

You have spoken over the next generation.
Over their lives.
Over their future.

Your words have become covering.
Your declarations have become seeds.

And what you have spoken—
Will not return empty.

You are not just living for today.

You are building legacy.

And as you continue—
You will begin to see the fruit
Of what you have declared.

Prophetic Charge

My words build generations.
I speak life, purpose, and destiny.

Week 9:

Finances & Provision — Trusting God as Your Source

Anchor Scripture (KJV)

"But my God shall supply all your need according to his riches in glory by Christ Jesus."
— *Philippians 4:19*

EXHORTATION

PART 1

Provision is not just about money.

It is about source.

Where you look for supply
Will determine how you live.

If your source is limited—
Your thinking becomes limited.

But God is not limited.

He is your provider.

EXHORTATION

PART 2

There may be moments of lack.
Moments of uncertainty.
Moments where things do not seem enough.

But lack does not define your life—
God does.

Provision is not always immediate—
But it is always available.

And as you trust Him,
You begin to see differently.

EXHORTATION

PART 3

This week is about alignment.

Aligning your mindset.
Aligning your faith.
Aligning your actions.

You are not called to live in fear of lack.
You are called to walk in trust.

And as you do—
Provision will follow alignment.

WEEKLY PROPHETIC PRAYER

Father, in the name of Jesus,

I acknowledge You as my source.

Remove every fear of lack.
Break every mindset of limitation.

Teach me to trust You completely.
Guide me in wisdom and stewardship.

Let provision flow into every area of my life.

In Jesus' name,
Amen.

WEEKLY AFFIRMATION

God is my source.
I am provided for in every area of my life.

Day 57

God is My Provider

Scripture (KJV)

"The Lord is my shepherd; I shall not want."
— *Psalm 23:1*

Reflection

Provision begins with understanding.

God is not just someone who gives—
He is your source.

When you truly believe that,
Fear begins to lose its power.

Because your supply
Is not dependent on one channel.

It is connected to Him.

Prophetic Declaration

I declare that God is my provider.

I lack nothing.
I am sustained.
I am supported.

My life is supplied by God.

Prayer

Father, help me to trust You as my provider.

Remove fear and uncertainty
And replace it with confidence.

In Jesus' name,
Amen.

Reflection Question

Do I truly see God as my source—or do I rely on other things?

Day 58

Breaking the Mindset of Lack

Scripture (KJV)

"And God is able to make all grace abound toward you…"
— *2 Corinthians 9:8*

Reflection

Lack often begins in the mind.

Before it shows in life—
It settles in thinking.

"I don't have enough."
"It will not work."
"There is no way."

These thoughts limit possibility.

But God is able.

Your situation is not the limit—
Your thinking might be.

Prophetic Declaration

I declare that every mindset of lack is broken.

I think with faith.
I believe in provision.

I am not limited—
God is able.

Prayer

Father, renew my mind.

Remove every limiting belief
And replace it with truth.

In Jesus' name,
Amen.

Reflection Question

What thoughts have been limiting my belief in provision?

Day 59

Wisdom in Finances

Scripture (KJV)

"The blessing of the Lord, it maketh rich, and he addeth no sorrow with it."
— *Proverbs 10:22*

Reflection

Provision is not only about receiving—
It is also about managing.

Wisdom matters.

How you handle what you have
Determines what you can sustain.

God gives provision—
But He also gives wisdom.

And when both are present—
There is stability.

Prophetic Declaration

I declare that I walk in financial wisdom.

I manage well.
I steward wisely.

I make decisions
That lead to stability and growth.

Prayer

Father, give me wisdom.

Help me to manage what I have
In a way that honors You.

In Jesus' name,
Amen.

Reflection Question

Am I handling my finances with wisdom?

Day 60

Provision in Difficult Times

Scripture (KJV)

"And the barrel of meal wasted not, neither did the cruse of oil fail…"
— *1 Kings 17:16*

Reflection

There are seasons that feel tight.

Moments when resources seem limited.
When things do not look like enough.

But God is not limited by what you see.

Even in difficult times—
He provides.

Provision does not always come in abundance first.
Sometimes it comes in consistency.

And what He sustains—
Will not fail.

Prophetic Declaration

I declare that I am provided for in every season.

Even in difficult times,
I do not lack.

God sustains me.
God supplies me.

Prayer

Father, in every season, be my provider.

When things feel uncertain,
Remind me that You are faithful.

In Jesus' name,
Amen.

Reflection Question

How do I respond when provision feels limited?

Day 61

Generosity

Scripture (KJV)

"Give, and it shall be given unto you…"
— *Luke 6:38*

Reflection

Generosity is not about how much you have—
It is about how you give.

It is a posture of the heart.

When you give,
You are not losing—
You are positioning yourself.

Giving reflects trust.

Trust that what you release
God is able to replenish.

Prophetic Declaration

I declare that I am generous.

I give freely and with wisdom.
I do not hold back in fear.

As I give,
I receive.

Prayer

Father, teach me to give.

Help me to be generous
With wisdom and faith.

In Jesus' name,
Amen.

Reflection Question

Do I give from fear—or from trust?

Day 62

Open Doors

Scripture (KJV)

"I have set before thee an open door, and no man can shut it…"
— *Revelation 3:8*

Reflection

Provision is not always money.

Sometimes, it is opportunity.

A door opening.
A connection forming.
A path becoming clear.

God provides through doors.

And what He opens—
Cannot be closed by man.

You are not stuck.
You are positioned.

Prophetic Declaration

I declare that doors are opening for me.

Opportunities are aligning.
Paths are becoming clear.

What God has opened
Cannot be shut.

Prayer

Father, open the right doors.

Guide me into opportunities
That align with Your will.

In Jesus' name,
Amen.

Reflection Question

Am I recognizing the opportunities God is placing before me?

Day 63

Overflow

Scripture (KJV)

"…I am come that they might have life, and that they might have it more abundantly."
—*John 10:10*

Reflection

God does not just provide enough—
He provides more than enough.

Not always immediately—
But through alignment,
Through growth,
Through faith.

Overflow is not just for you.

It positions you to bless others.
To give.
To support.

You are not meant to live in lack.
You are meant to live in abundance.

Prophetic Declaration

I declare that I walk in overflow.

I have more than enough.
I am blessed to be a blessing.

My life reflects abundance
In every area.

Prayer

Father, lead me into overflow.

Not just for myself—
But so I can be a blessing to others.

In Jesus' name,
Amen.

Reflection Question

Do I believe that abundance is possible for me?

WEEK 9 CLOSING

You have completed Week 9.

You have shifted your thinking.
You have strengthened your trust.

You no longer see provision
As something uncertain.

You see God as your source.

You have learned to:
Trust,
Give,
Manage,
And expect.

And as you continue—
You will walk in confidence,
Not fear.

Because provision is no longer a question.

It is established.

Prophetic Charge

God is my source.
I walk in provision and abundance.

Week 10:

Health & Wholeness — Caring for the Whole Woman

Anchor Scripture (KJV)

"Beloved, I wish above all things that thou mayest prosper and be in health, even as thy soul prospereth."
— *3 John 1:2*

EXHORTATION

PART 1

Health is not only physical.

It is emotional.
It is mental.
It is spiritual.

You can look well outwardly
And still feel unsettled within.

But God's desire is not partial wellness—
It is wholeness.

EXHORTATION

PART 2

Wholeness means balance.

A sound mind.
A steady heart.
A body that is cared for.

It is not perfection—
It is alignment.

You are not meant to live overwhelmed,
Exhausted, or constantly unsettled.

There is a better way.

EXHORTATION

PART 3

This week is about restoration.

Restoring peace.
Restoring strength.
Restoring balance.

You will learn to:
Care for yourself,
Guard your mind,
And walk in health.

Because your well-being matters.

WEEKLY PROPHETIC PRAYER

Father, in the name of Jesus,

I receive wholeness.

Heal my body.
Restore my emotions.
Strengthen my mind.

Where there has been stress, bring peace.
Where there has been weakness, bring strength.

Let every part of my life align with Your peace.

In Jesus' name,
Amen.

WEEKLY AFFIRMATION

I am whole.
I walk in health, peace, and balance.

Day 64

Health in the Body

Scripture (KJV)

"He sent his word, and healed them…"
— *Psalm 107:20*

Reflection

Your body matters.

It carries you.
Supports you.
Serves you daily.

And it deserves care.

Health is not something to neglect—
It is something to steward.

God's Word carries power.
Even for your physical body.

Healing is not distant—
It is available.

Prophetic Declaration

I declare that my body is healthy.

I receive healing and strength.
My body functions as it was designed.

I walk in divine health.

Prayer

Father, I receive healing.

Touch my body.
Restore strength.

Let my health align with Your will.

In Jesus' name,
Amen.

Reflection Question

Am I taking care of my body intentionally?

Day 65

A Sound Mind

Scripture (KJV)

"For God hath not given us the spirit of fear; but of power, and of love, and of a sound mind."
— *2 Timothy 1:7*

Reflection

Your mind is powerful.

It processes,
Responds,
And directs your life.

But if left unchecked,
It can become overwhelmed.

Fear, worry, and stress
Can cloud your thinking.

But you have been given a sound mind.

Clarity is available.
Peace is possible.

Prophetic Declaration

I declare that I have a sound mind.

I am not overwhelmed.
I am not confused.

My thoughts are clear.
My mind is stable and at peace.

Prayer

Father, stabilize my mind.

Remove every form of anxiety
And replace it with peace.

In Jesus' name,
Amen.

Reflection Question

What thoughts have been affecting my peace?

Day 66

Emotional Balance

Scripture (KJV)

"Let the peace of God rule in your hearts…"
— *Colossians 3:15*

Reflection

Emotions are real.

But they are not meant to control you.

There will be highs.
There will be lows.

But balance is possible.

Peace stabilizes emotions.
It helps you respond—not react.

You are not at the mercy of your feelings.
You are guided by truth.

Prophetic Declaration

I declare that my emotions are balanced.

I am not controlled by how I feel.
I walk in peace and stability.

My heart is calm and steady.

Prayer

Father, bring balance to my emotions.

Help me to remain steady
In every situation.

In Jesus' name,
Amen.

Reflection Question

Do my emotions control me—or do I remain grounded?

Day 67

Rest and Renewal

Scripture (KJV)

"Come unto me, all ye that labour and are heavy laden, and I will give you rest."
— *Matthew 11:28*

Reflection

Rest is necessary.

Not just sleep—
But true rest.

A release from pressure.
A pause from striving.
A moment to breathe.

Many people continue without rest
And slowly become overwhelmed.

But God invites you to rest.

In His presence—
There is renewal.

Prophetic Declaration

I declare that I receive rest.

I release every burden.
I let go of pressure.

I am renewed in God's presence.

Prayer

Father, give me rest.

Help me to pause,
To release,
And to be renewed.

In Jesus' name,
Amen.

Reflection Question

Am I allowing myself to truly rest?

Day 68

Freedom from Stress

Scripture (KJV)

"Casting all your care upon him; for he careth for you."
— *1 Peter 5:7*

Reflection

Stress builds quietly.

Responsibilities, expectations, pressure—
They accumulate.

And before you realize it,
You feel overwhelmed.

But you were not created to carry everything.

You can release it.

God cares about what concerns you.
Nothing is too small.
Nothing is too heavy.

Prophetic Declaration

I declare that I am free from stress.

I release every burden.
I do not carry what is not mine to carry.

I walk in peace.

Prayer

Father, I release every concern to You.

Help me to let go
Of what is weighing me down.

In Jesus' name,
Amen.

Reflection Question

What am I holding onto that I need to release?

Day 69

Inner Peace

Scripture (KJV)

"Peace I leave with you, my peace I give unto you…"
— *John 14:27*

Reflection

Peace is not external.

It does not depend on everything going right.

It is internal.

It remains
Even when things are uncertain.

Even when situations are unresolved.

You can carry peace
Into every situation.

Because it comes from God.

Prophetic Declaration

I declare that I walk in inner peace.

My heart is calm.
My mind is steady.

I am not disturbed—
I am grounded in peace.

Prayer

Father, fill me with Your peace.

Let it settle within me
And remain in every situation.

In Jesus' name,
Amen.

Reflection Question

What is trying to disturb my peace?

Day 70

Strength and Vitality

Scripture (KJV)

"The Lord will give strength unto his people…"
— *Psalm 29:11*

Reflection

Strength is not just endurance—
It is vitality.

Energy.
Ability.
Capacity.

You are not meant to move through life
Constantly drained.

God strengthens you.

He restores what has been depleted.
He renews your capacity.

You can move forward with strength.

Prophetic Declaration

I declare that I am strong and energized.

My body is strengthened.
My spirit is refreshed.

I move through life with vitality and strength.

Prayer

Father, strengthen me.

Restore my energy.
Renew my capacity.

Help me to move forward with strength.

In Jesus' name,
Amen.

Reflection Question

Where do I need renewed strength and energy?

WEEK 10 CLOSING

You have completed Week 10.

You have slowed down.
You have released.
You have received.

Your body is being restored.
Your mind is being stabilized.
Your emotions are being balanced.

You are no longer carrying everything alone.

You are learning to rest.
To release.
To renew.

And as you continue—
You will walk with greater peace,
Greater strength,
And greater clarity.

Because wholeness is not distant.
It is becoming your reality.

Prophetic Charge

I am whole.
I walk in health, peace, and strength.

Week 11:

Spiritual Authority & Growth — Walking in Power and Maturity

Anchor Scripture (KJV)

"Behold, I give unto you power… over all the power of the enemy…"
— *Luke 10:19*

EXHORTATION

PART 1

Spiritual growth is intentional.

It does not happen automatically.
It happens through pursuit.

Through prayer.
Through the Word.
Through consistency.

The more you grow—
The more you understand who you are.

EXHORTATION

PART 2

Authority is not something you chase.

It is something you walk in
When you know your position.

You are not powerless.
You are not without influence.

You have been given authority.

Over fear.
Over confusion.
Over every opposing force.

EXHORTATION

PART 3

This week is about stepping into that authority.

Speaking with confidence.
Standing with conviction.
Growing with intention.

You are not meant to remain at the same level.

You are growing.

And as you grow—
You begin to walk differently.

WEEKLY PROPHETIC PRAYER

Father, in the name of Jesus,

I step into the authority You have given me.

Strengthen my spirit.
Deepen my understanding.
Increase my growth.

Help me to walk in confidence
And to live with awareness of who I am in You.

In Jesus' name,
Amen.

WEEKLY AFFIRMATION

I walk in spiritual authority.
I am growing daily in strength and understanding.

Day 71

Knowing Who You Are

Scripture (KJV)

"Ye are of God, little children, and have overcome them…"
— *1 John 4:4*

Reflection

Authority begins with identity.

If you do not know who you are,
You will not walk in what you have.

You are not weak.
You are not powerless.

You belong to God.

And because of that—
You have overcome.

Prophetic Declaration

I declare that I know who I am.

I am not confused.
I am not uncertain.

I am rooted in my identity in God.

Prayer

Father, help me to understand who I am.

Let my identity be clear
And established in You.

In Jesus' name,
Amen.

Reflection Question

Do I truly understand my identity in God?

Day 72

Walking in Authority

Scripture (KJV)

"Behold, I give unto you power…"
— *Luke 10:19*

Reflection

Authority is not about control.

It is about position.

You have been given authority—
Not to dominate people,
But to stand firm spiritually.

You do not have to shrink.
You do not have to hesitate.

You can walk confidently.

Prophetic Declaration

I declare that I walk in authority.

I am confident.
I am bold.
I stand firm in who I am.

Prayer

Father, help me to walk in authority.

Remove hesitation
And replace it with confidence.

In Jesus' name,
Amen.

Reflection Question

Where do I need to walk more confidently in my authority?

Day 73

Growth Through the Word

Scripture (KJV)

"Thy word is a lamp unto my feet, and a light unto my path."
— *Psalm 119:105*

Reflection

Growth requires input.

What you feed your spirit
Determines how you grow.

The Word of God brings clarity.
Direction.
Understanding.

Without it, growth is limited.

With it, growth is steady.

Prophetic Declaration

I declare that I grow through the Word.

I am guided.
I am strengthened.
I am established in truth.

Prayer

Father, help me to grow in Your Word.

Let it guide me
And strengthen me daily.

In Jesus' name,
Amen.

Reflection Question

Am I feeding my spirit consistently?

Day 74

A Strong Prayer Life

Scripture (KJV)

"Pray without ceasing."
— *1 Thessalonians 5:17*

Reflection

Prayer is not just an activity—
It is connection.

A continuous awareness of God.
A conversation that does not end.

It is not about long words—
It is about consistent presence.

When your prayer life is strong,
You are not easily shaken.

Because you remain connected.

Prophetic Declaration

I declare that my prayer life is strong.

I remain connected to God daily.
I do not drift—I stay aligned.

Prayer is a consistent part of my life.

Prayer

Father, draw me closer.

Help me to remain connected
And to build a consistent prayer life.

In Jesus' name,
Amen.

Reflection Question

How consistent is my prayer life?

Day 75

Spiritual Awareness

Scripture (KJV)

"Watch and pray…"
— *Matthew 26:41*

Reflection

Awareness matters.

Not everything is physical.
Some things are spiritual.

Being aware helps you:
Discern,
Respond,
And stay aligned.

You are not called to live unaware.

You are called to be alert,
Grounded,
And discerning.

Prophetic Declaration

I declare that I am spiritually aware.

I see clearly.
I discern correctly.

I remain alert and aligned with God.

Prayer

Father, sharpen my awareness.

Help me to see clearly
And to discern accurately.

In Jesus' name,
Amen.

Reflection Question

Am I aware of what is happening around me spiritually?

Day 76

Consistency in Growth

Scripture (KJV)

"But grow in grace, and in the knowledge of our Lord…"
— *2 Peter 3:18*

Reflection

Growth is not occasional—
It is consistent.

Small daily steps
Lead to lasting change.

It is not about doing everything at once—
It is about staying steady.

When you remain consistent,
Growth becomes visible.

Prophetic Declaration

I declare that I grow consistently.

I do not start and stop.
I remain steady.

My growth is continuous and visible.

Prayer

Father, help me to remain consistent.

Give me discipline
To continue growing daily.

In Jesus' name,
Amen.

Reflection Question

Am I consistent in my spiritual growth?

Day 77

Living in Authority

Scripture (KJV)

"Ye are the light of the world…"
— *Matthew 5:14*

Reflection

Authority is not something you visit—
It is something you live in.

Daily.

In how you speak.
In how you respond.
In how you carry yourself.

You are not meant to go in and out of confidence.

You are meant to remain.

You are the light.

And light does not hide.

Prophetic Declaration

I declare that I live in authority.

I walk confidently.
I stand firmly.

I do not shrink—
I shine.

Prayer

Father, help me to live in authority.

Let my life reflect confidence
And alignment with You.

In Jesus' name,
Amen.

Reflection Question

Am I consistently walking in authority—or only occasionally?

WEEK 11 CLOSING

You have completed Week 11.

You have grown.
You have strengthened.
You have stepped into authority.

You are no longer uncertain.

You are aware.
You are grounded.
You are confident.

You have learned to:
Pray,
Discern,
Grow,
And stand.

And as you continue—
You will walk with greater clarity,
Greater confidence,
And greater strength.

Because authority is no longer something you are learning.

It is something you are living.

Prophetic Charge

I walk in authority.
I grow daily in strength and power.

Week 12:

Victory & Dominion — Living Above and Not Beneath

Anchor Scripture (KJV)

"Nay, in all these things we are more than conquerors through him that loved us."
— *Romans 8:37*

EXHORTATION

PART 1

Victory is not something you chase.

It is something you walk in.

Because of who you are in God,
You are not fighting for victory—
You are living from it.

EXHORTATION

PART 2

There will always be challenges.

But challenges do not define your outcome.

They reveal your position.

You are not defeated.
You are not overcome.

You are more than a conqueror.

EXHORTATION

PART 3

This week is about living above.

Above fear.
Above limitation.
Above every voice that tries to reduce you.

You are not beneath circumstances—
You have dominion.

And as you walk in it—
You begin to see differently.

WEEKLY PROPHETIC PRAYER

Father, in the name of Jesus,

I step into victory.

I reject defeat.
I reject limitation.
I reject every lie that says I am less.

I walk in authority.
I walk in confidence.
I walk in dominion.

Let my life reflect victory in every area.

In Jesus' name,
Amen.

WEEKLY AFFIRMATION

I am victorious.
I walk in dominion in every area of my life.

Day 78

More Than a Conqueror

Scripture (KJV)

"Nay, in all these things we are more than conquerors…"
— *Romans 8:37*

Reflection

You are not just surviving.

You are overcoming.

A conqueror wins—
But more than a conqueror lives in victory.

You do not have to struggle to prove yourself.

Victory has already been established.

You are walking in what has already been secured.

Prophetic Declaration

I declare that I am more than a conqueror.

I do not live in defeat.
I walk in victory.

I overcome every challenge
Through God.

Prayer

Father, help me to walk in victory.

Let me see myself
As You see me.

In Jesus' name,
Amen.

Reflection Question

Do I live like I am victorious—or do I still think like I am struggling?

Day 79

Dominion Over Circumstances

Scripture (KJV)

"And God said… have dominion…"
— *Genesis 1:28*

Reflection

Dominion means authority.

Not control over everything—
But authority in how you respond.

Circumstances will come.
Situations will arise.

But they do not control you.

You have the ability to stand above.

Prophetic Declaration

I declare that I have dominion.

I am not controlled by circumstances.
I respond with authority.

I walk above and not beneath.

Prayer

Father, help me to walk in dominion.

Let me respond with strength
And not react in fear.

In Jesus' name,
Amen.

Reflection Question

Do I allow situations to control me—or do I stand above them?

Day 80

Overcoming Every Challenge

Scripture (KJV)

"No weapon that is formed against thee shall prosper…"
— *Isaiah 54:17*

Reflection

Challenges are part of life.

But they are not your end.

What comes against you
Does not determine your outcome.

God covers you.
Protects you.
Strengthens you.

You are not without defense.

You are not without help.

Prophetic Declaration

I declare that I overcome every challenge.

Nothing formed against me will prosper.
I am protected.
I am strengthened.

I move forward with confidence.

Prayer

Father, strengthen me in every challenge.

Help me to stand firm
And to trust in Your covering.

In Jesus' name,
Amen.

Reflection Question

How do I respond when challenges arise?

Day 81

Living Above Limitation

Scripture (KJV)

"I can do all things through Christ which strengtheneth me."
— *Philippians 4:13*

Reflection

Limitation often begins in the mind.

What you believe
Shapes what you attempt.

If you see yourself as limited—
You will live that way.

But you are not limited.

Through God—
You are capable.

Prophetic Declaration

I declare that I live above limitation.

I do not think small.
I do not live restricted.

I walk in ability and confidence.

Prayer

Father, remove every limiting belief.

Help me to see possibilities
And walk in them.

In Jesus' name,
Amen.

Reflection Question

What belief has been limiting me?

Day 82

Confidence in Victory

Scripture (KJV)

"The Lord is my light and my salvation; whom shall I fear?"
— *Psalm 27:1*

Reflection

Confidence is not arrogance.

It is assurance.

You are not hoping things will work—
You are confident they will.

Because your confidence
Is not in yourself alone.

It is in God.

Prophetic Declaration

I declare that I am confident.

I do not fear.
I do not hesitate.

I walk boldly in victory.

Prayer

Father, strengthen my confidence.

Help me to walk without fear
And to trust You completely.

In Jesus' name,
Amen.

Reflection Question

Do I walk with confidence—or hesitation?

Day 83

Established in Victory

Scripture (KJV)

"The Lord shall establish thee an holy people unto himself…"
— *Deuteronomy 28:9*

Reflection

Victory is not temporary.

It is established.

It becomes your way of living.

You do not go in and out of victory—
You remain in it.

You are rooted.

You are grounded.

You are established.

Prophetic Declaration

I declare that I am established in victory.

I do not move in and out.
I remain steady.

Victory is my lifestyle.

Prayer

Father, establish me.

Let my life reflect stability and victory
In every area.

In Jesus' name,
Amen.

Reflection Question

Do I remain steady—or do I fluctuate?

Day 84

Walking in Dominion Daily

Scripture (KJV)

"Be strong and of a good courage…"
— *Joshua 1:9*

Reflection

This is where it all comes together.

Everything you have learned—
You now live.

Not occasionally—
But daily.

You are not going back.

You are moving forward—
With confidence, clarity, and strength.

Prophetic Declaration

I declare that I walk in dominion daily.

I am strong.
I am confident.
I am aligned.

I live in victory in every area of my life.

Prayer

Father, help me to walk daily in what I have learned.

Let my life reflect growth, strength, and victory.

In Jesus' name,
Amen.

Reflection Question

Am I ready to live daily in victory?

FINAL CLOSING CHARGE

You have completed this journey.

But this is not the end.

It is the beginning.

You are not the same.

You have grown.
You have healed.
You have aligned.

You now carry:
Clarity.
Strength.
Confidence.
Authority.

Everything you have declared—
Has taken root.

And what has taken root—
Will produce fruit.

Do not go back.

Do not shrink.

Do not forget who you are.

You are a prophetic woman.

You speak life.
You walk in truth.
You live in victory.

FINAL PROPHETIC CHARGE

I am who God says I am.
I walk in purpose, strength, and victory.

My life is aligned.
My voice carries power.

And I will continue to become
Everything God has called me to be.

Final Prayer

A Prayer of Alignment, Strength, and Victory

Father, in the name of Jesus,

I thank You for this journey.

Thank You for every word spoken,
Every truth revealed,
Every place within me that has been touched.

Today, I stand different.

Not because everything around me has changed—
But because something within me has.

I align myself fully with You.

Let every word I have declared
Take root in my life.

Let it grow.
Let it produce fruit.
Let it become my reality.

Where there was confusion—
I receive clarity.

Where there was weakness—
I receive strength.

Where there was fear—
I receive boldness.

Where there was limitation—
I receive expansion.

I refuse to go back.

I refuse to shrink.

I refuse to forget who I am.

I walk in identity.
I walk in healing.
I walk in faith.
I walk in purpose.
I walk in strength.
I walk in wisdom.
I walk in wholeness.
I walk in authority.
I walk in victory.

Everything connected to me aligns.

My life aligns.
My family aligns.
My future aligns.

Let my voice carry power.

Let my life reflect Your truth.

Let everything I have received
Be established in me.

From this day forward,
I move with confidence,
Clarity,
And strength.

I am not the same.

I am transformed.

And I will continue to become
Everything You have called me to be.

In Jesus' name,
Amen.

About the Author

Prophetess Dr. Racheal Odoy is a prophetic voice, author, entrepreneur, and transformational speaker with a deep passion for restoring identity, healing hearts, and empowering individuals to walk in their God-given purpose.

With a unique blend of prophetic insight, practical teaching, and spiritual depth, she ministers to women and audiences globally—helping them rise above limitation, overcome life's challenges, and step into lives of clarity, strength, and victory.

She holds a Bachelor's Degree in Social Work and Social Administration, a background in Journalism and Mass Communication, and a Doctor of Philosophy in Christian Leadership and Business.

Dr. Odoy is the co-founder of No-Limits International Christian Center and the founder of outreach initiatives dedicated to supporting widows, orphans, and underprivileged communities.

Through her books, teachings, and voice, she is committed to bringing healing, restoration, and transformation—helping people not only hear truth, but live it.

Dr. Odoy's books are available on Amazon and through her ministry platforms.

Stay Connected

Continue this journey beyond these pages.

For teachings, prophetic insights, and updates:

Website: *rachealodoyministries.com*
Follow on social media
Discover more books and resources

You are not meant to walk this journey alone.

A Final Invitation

If this book has spoken to you,
Encouraged you,
Or helped you grow—

Take a moment to respond.

Share it with someone who needs it.
Recommend it to a friend.
And consider leaving a review.

Your voice can help another woman
Begin her journey.

Do not let this be the end.

Continue declaring.
Continue growing.
Continue becoming.

You are not the same.

You are stronger.
You are clearer.
You are aligned.

Final Reminder

You are a prophetic woman.

Your words carry power.
Your life carries purpose.
And your future is aligned with God.

www.ingramcontent.com/pod-product-compliance
Lightning Source LLC
LaVergne TN
LVHW020708110826
845149LV00012B/2159

* 9 7 9 8 9 8 9 8 0 9 8 9 9 *